YOU ARE IN MY HEART

You Are in My Heart

Wisdom for a New Generation

POPE FRANCIS

EDITED BY

Mark-David Janus, CSP

NOVALIS
Toronto, Canada

Paulist Press
New York / Mahwah, NJ

Published by Paulist Press
997 Macarthur Boulevard
Mahwah, NJ 07430
www.paulistpress.com

Cover image copyright © Servizio Fotografico—
L'Osservatore Romano
Cover and book design by Lynn Else

Compilation copyright © 2018 by Paulist Press

Library of Congress Cataloging-in-Publication Data is available
upon request.

ISBN 978-0-8091-5410-4 (paperback)
ISBN 978-1-58768-790-7 (e-book)

Published in Canada by Novalis
Publishing Office   Head Office
10 Lower Spadina Ave., Suite 400   4475 Frontenac St.
Toronto, Ontario, Canada   Montreal, Quebec, Canada
M5V 2Z2   H2H 2S2
www.novalis.ca

ISBN: 978-2-89688-590-9
Cataloguing in Publication is available from Library and
Archives Canada.
We acknowledge the support of the Government of Canada.

Printed and bound in Canada

"I wanted you to be the centre of attention, because you are in my heart," Pope Francis wrote to young people when announcing that he was calling the bishops of the world to meet in a synod in 2018 to discuss "Young People, the Faith and Vocational Discernment." What follows in this little book is from Pope Francis's heart; words he has addressed to young people around the world during his first five years as pope. "I invite you to hear God's voice resounding in your heart through the breath of the Holy Spirit," says Pope Francis. May his words help you hear God's voice resounding in your heart.

Contents

Part 3: Vocation

PART 1

A Joy to Be Young

Love

LOVE

What is the most important lesson that you have to learn in life? It is learning how to love. This is the challenge which life sets before you today: learning how to love.

True joy does not come from things or from possessing, no! It is born from the encounter, from the relationship with others, it is born from feeling accepted, understood and loved, and from accepting, from understanding and from loving; and this is not because of a passing fancy but because the other is a person.

True love is both loving and letting oneself be loved. It is harder to let ourselves be loved than it is to love. That is why it is so hard to achieve the perfect love of God, because we can love him but the important thing is to let ourselves be loved by him. True love is being open to that love which was there first and catches us by surprise. If all you have is information, you are closed to surprises. Love makes you open to surprises. Love is always a surprise because it starts with a dialogue between two persons: the one who loves and the one who is loved. We say that God is the God of surprises because he always loved us first, and he waits to take us by surprise. God surprises us. Let's allow ourselves to be surprised by God.

Dear young people, the heart of the human being aspires to great things, lofty values, deep friendships, ties that are strengthened rather than broken by the trials of life. The human being aspires to love and to be loved. This is our deepest aspiration: to love and be loved; and definitively.

You and your friends are giving and giving, helping other people. But what about you? Do you let them give something to you?…How many young people like you here today know how to give, but have not yet learned how to receive?

I would like to speak especially to you young people: be committed to your daily duties, your studies, your work, to relationships of friendship, to helping others; your future also depends on how you live these precious years of your life. Do not be afraid of commitment, of sacrifice and do not view the future with fear. Keep your hope alive: there is always a light on the horizon.

LOVE

If you are really open to the deepest
aspirations of your hearts, you
will realize that you possess an
unquenchable thirst for happiness.

Joy is born from the gratuitousness of an
encounter! It is hearing someone say,
but not necessarily with words: "You are
important to me." This is beautiful....And
it is these very words that God makes us
understand. In calling you, God says to you:
"You are important to me, I love you, I am
counting on you."

Hope

HOPE

But I will tell you one thing: Do you
know where the future is? It is in
your heart. It is in your mind and in
your hands. If you feel good, if you
think hard and if you carry forward
these good thoughts and good
feelings with your hands, the future
will be better. The future is for
young people.

Why do I like being with young people? Because you have the promise of hope in your heart. You are bearers of hope.

H
O
P
E

Dear young people, do not be discouraged. It is easy to say this, but please make an effort not to be discouraged. With the help of God, continue to hope in a better future, despite the difficulties and obstacles which you are currently facing.

Young people, please: don't put yourselves
at the tail end of history. Be active members!
Go on the offensive! Play down the field,
build a better world, a world of brothers and
sisters, a world of justice, of love, of peace,
of fraternity, of solidarity. Play always on
the offensive!

Do well the routine things of every day and all the daily actions, tasks, meetings with people; doing the little everyday things with a great heart open to God and to others.

A young heart that welcomes Christ's love becomes hope for others, it is an immense force! But you, boys and girls, all young people, you must transform us and yourselves into hope! Open the doors to a new world of hope. This is your task.

I hope that you will always realize
that true happiness comes from
helping others, giving ourselves to
them in self-sacrifice, mercy and
compassion. In this way you will
be a powerful force for the renewal
of society, not only in the work
of restoring buildings but more
importantly, in building up God's
kingdom of holiness, justice and
peace in your native land.

Negativity is contagious but so is positivity; desperation is contagious but so is joy: do not follow negative people but continue to radiate light and hope around you!

You and your friends are filled with the optimism, energy and good will which are so characteristic of this period of life. Let Christ turn your natural optimism into Christian hope, your energy into moral virtue, your good will into genuine self-sacrificing love! This is the path you are called to take. This is the path to overcoming all that threatens hope, virtue and love in your lives and in your culture. In this way your youth will be a gift to Jesus and to the world.

Youth is for taking risks—good risks, risks full of hope. It is meant to be staked on great things. Youth is meant to be given away, to help others to know the Lord. Don't keep your youth to yourselves: get out there!

Faith

F
A
I
T
H

Your families and local communities have passed on to you the great gift of faith, Christ has grown in you. Today he desires to come here to confirm you in this faith, faith in the living Christ who dwells within you, but I have come as well to be confirmed by the enthusiasm of your faith!

Today…every day, but today in a particular way, Jesus is sowing the seed. When we accept the word of God, then we are the Field of Faith! Please, let Christ and his word enter your life; let the seed of the Word of God enter, let it blossom, and let it grow. God will take care of everything, but let him work in you and bring about this growth.

Let us all look into our hearts and
each one of us tell Jesus that we
want to receive the seed of his Word.
Say to him: Jesus, look upon the
stones, the thorns, and the weeds
that I have, but also look upon this
small piece of ground that I offer
to you so that the seed may enter
my heart. In silence, let us allow the
seed of Jesus to enter our hearts.
Remember this moment. Everyone
knows the seed that has been
received. Allow it to grow, and God
will nurture it.

Faith in Jesus leads to a hope that goes further, to a certainty based not on our qualities and skills alone, but on the word of God, on the invitation that comes from him. Without making too many human calculations and without worrying about checking whether the situation that surrounds you coincides with your points of security. Put out into the deep, go out for yourselves: go out of our small world and open ourselves to God, to open ourselves increasingly also to our brethren.

This is our faith in the true presence of Jesus Christ, true God and true Man, in the consecrated Bread and Wine, is authentic if we commit ourselves to *walk behind Him and with Him*. To adore and to walk: a people who adore are a people who walk! Walk with Him and behind Him, as we seek to practice *His* Commandment, the one he gave the disciples precisely at the Last Supper: "Even as I have loved you, that you also love one another" (John 13:34). People who adore God in the Eucharist are people who walk in charity. To adore God in the Eucharist, to walk with God in fraternal charity.

The People of God is *a disciple People*—
because it receives the faith—and *a
missionary People*—because it transmits the
faith. And this is what Baptism works in us: it
gives us Grace and hands on the faith to us.
All of us in the Church are disciples, and this
we are forever, our whole lifelong; and we are
all missionaries, each in the place the Lord
has assigned to him or her. Everyone: the
littlest one is also a missionary.

Today's Gospel passage also asks each
of us, is your faith good? Each one
answer in his or her heart. Is my faith
good? How does the Lord find our
hearts? A heart that is firm as a rock,
or a heart like sand, that is doubtful,
diffident, disbelieving? It will do us
good to think about this throughout
the day today. If the Lord finds in our
heart, I don't say a perfect, but sincere,
genuine faith, then He also sees in
us living stones with which to build
his community. This community's
foundation stone is Christ, the unique
cornerstone. On his side, Peter is the
rock, the visible foundation of the
Church's unity; but every baptized
person is called to offer Jesus his or
her lowly but sincere faith, so that He
may continue to build his Church,
today, in every part of the world.

On the Cross, Jesus is united with every person who suffers from hunger in a world which, on the other hand, permits itself the luxury of throwing away tons of food every day; on the Cross, Jesus is united to the many mothers and fathers who suffer as they see their children become victims of drug-induced euphoria; on the Cross, Jesus is united with those who are persecuted for their religion, for their beliefs or simply for the colour of their skin; on the Cross, Jesus is united with so many young people who have lost faith in political institutions, because they see in them only selfishness and corruption; he unites himself with those young people who have lost faith in the Church, or even in God because of the counter-witness of Christians and ministers of the Gospel.

What has the Cross left in each one of us? You see, it gives us a treasure that no one else can give: the certainty of the faithful love which God has for us. A love so great that it enters into our sin and forgives it, enters into our suffering and gives us the strength to bear it. It is a love which enters into death to conquer it and to save us.

You are called to care for creation not only
as responsible citizens, but also as followers
of Christ! Respect for the environment
means more than simply using cleaner
products or recycling what we use. These
are important aspects, but not enough. We
need to see, with the eyes of faith, the beauty
of God's saving plan, the link between the
natural environment and the dignity of the
human person. Men and women are made
in the image and likeness of God, and given
dominion over creation (cf. Gen 1:26–28).
As stewards of God's creation, we are called
to make the earth a beautiful garden for the
human family. When we destroy our forests,
ravage our soil and pollute our seas, we
betray that noble calling.

Do not be afraid to live out faith!
Be witnesses of Christ in your daily
environment, with simplicity and
courage. Above all may you be
able to show those you meet, your
peers, the Face of mercy and the
love of God who always forgives,
encourages and imbues hope.
May you always be attentive to the
other, especially to people who
are poorer and weaker, living and
bearing witness to brotherly love, to
counter all forms of selfishness and
withdrawal.

Young people must say to the world: to follow Christ is good; to go with Christ is good; the message of Christ is good; emerging from ourselves, to the ends of the earth and of existence, to take Jesus there, is good!

FAITH

These young people are from every continent, they speak many languages, they bring with them different cultures, and yet they also find in Christ the answer to their highest aspirations, held in common, and they can satisfy the hunger for a pure truth and an authentic love which binds them together in spite of differences.

Christ offers them space, knowing that there is no force more powerful than the one released from the hearts of young people when they have been conquered by the experience of friendship with him. Christ has confidence in young people and entrusts them with the very future of his mission, "Go and make disciples." Go beyond the confines of what is humanly possible and create a world of brothers and sisters! And young people have confidence in Christ: they are not afraid to risk for him the only life they have, because they know they will not be disappointed.

Listen! Young people are the window through which the future enters the world.

This is an effective image of the Church:
a boat which must brave the storms and
sometimes seems on the point of capsizing.
What saves her is not the skill and courage
of her crew members, but faith which allows
her to walk, even in the dark, amid hardships.
Faith gives us the certainty of Jesus' presence
always beside us, of his hand which grasps
us to pull us back from danger. We are all on
this boat, and we feel secure here despite our
limitations and our weaknesses. We are safe
especially when we are ready to kneel and
worship Jesus, the only Lord of our life.

In every one of these people who are victims of difficult situations, there is an image of God Who for various reasons has been mistreated and trampled. There is a history of pain, of sufferings that we cannot ignore. And this is the folly of faith.

The faithful and ready response to the Lord's call always enables one to achieve extraordinary things. But Jesus himself told us that we are capable of performing miracles with our faith, faith in Him, faith in his word, faith in his voice. Peter however begins to sink the moment he looks away from Jesus and he allows himself to be overwhelmed by the hardships around him. But the Lord is always there, and when Peter calls him, Jesus saves him from danger. Peter's character, with his passion and his weaknesses, can describe our faith: ever fragile and impoverished, anxious yet victorious, Christian faith walks to meet the Risen Lord, amid the world's storms and dangers.

Being Christian is not just obeying
orders but means being in Christ,
thinking like him, acting like him,
loving like him; it means letting
him take possession of our life and
change it, transform it, and free it
from the darkness of evil and sin.

Solidarity

SOLIDARITY

In life you can do two contrary things: build bridges or build walls. Walls separate, they divide. Bridges connect.

The culture of selfishness and individualism that often prevails in our society is not, I repeat, not what builds up and leads to a more habitable world: rather, it is the culture of solidarity that does so; the culture of solidarity means seeing others not as rivals or statistics, but brothers and sisters. And we are all brothers and sisters!

SOLIDARITY

All of us need to experience *a conversion in the way we see the poor*. We have to care for them and be sensitive to their spiritual and material needs.

By loving one another, learning to listen, to understand, to forgive, to be accepting and to help others, everybody, with no one excluded or ostracized. Dear young people, be true "athletes of Christ"!

SOLIDARITY

What we are called to respect in each person is first of all his life, his physical integrity, his dignity and the rights deriving from that dignity, his reputation, his property, his ethnic and cultural identity, his ideas and his political choices. We are therefore called to think, speak and write respectfully of the other, not only in his presence, but always and everywhere, avoiding unfair criticism or defamation.

The Pope loves everyone, rich and poor alike, but he is obliged in the name of Christ to remind all that the rich must help, respect and promote the poor. I exhort you to generous solidarity and to the return of economics and finance to an ethical approach which favours human beings.

SOLIDARITY

How many young people renounce
their own interests in order to
dedicate themselves to children,
the disabled, the elderly....They are
martyrs too! Daily martyrs, martyrs
of everyday life!

Cultivating and caring for creation is an instruction of God which he gave not only at the beginning of history, but has also given to each one of us; it is part of his plan; it means making the world increase with responsibility, transforming it so that it may be a garden, an inhabitable place for us all.

SOLIDARITY

Freedom means being able to think about what we do, being able to assess what is good and what is bad, these are the types of conduct that lead to development; it means always opting for the good. Let us be free for goodness. And in this do not be afraid to go against the tide, even if it is not easy!

You young people, my dear young friends, you have a particular sensitivity towards injustice, but you are often disappointed by facts that speak of corruption on the part of people who put their own interests before the common good. To you and to all, I repeat: never yield to discouragement, do not lose trust, do not allow your hope to be extinguished.

SOLIDARITY

No matter how much or how little we have individually, each one of us is called to personally reach out and serve our brothers and sisters in need. There is always someone near us who is in need, materially, emotionally, spiritually. The greatest gift we can give to them is our friendship, our concern, our tenderness, our love for Jesus.

Anyone who is Christian has a duty to
bear witness to the Gospel: to protect life
courageously and lovingly in all its phases.
I encourage you to do this always with
closeness, proximity: so that every woman
may feel respected as a person, heard,
accepted and supported.

SOLIDARITY

Peace builds bridges, whereas hatred is the builder of walls. You must decide, in life: either I will make bridges or I will make walls. Walls divide and hatred grows: when there is division, hatred grows.

Bridges unite, and when there is a bridge hatred can go away, because I can hear the other and speak with the other. When you shake the hand of a friend, of a person, you make a human bridge.

SOLIDARITY

When you strike someone, when you insult another person, you build a wall. Hatred always grows with walls.

At times, it may happen that you want to make a bridge and you offer your hand, but the other party does not take it; these are the humiliations that we must suffer in life in order to do good.

SOLIDARITY

Creation is not a good to be exploited but a gift to look after. Ecological commitment itself affords an opportunity for new concern in the sectors linked to it, such as energy, and the prevention and removal of different forms of pollution....May caring for creation, and looking after man through dignified work be a common task!

Everybody, according to his or her particular opportunities and responsibilities, should be able to make a personal contribution to putting an end to so many social injustices.

SOLIDARITY

I want to encourage you, as Christian citizens…, to offer yourselves passionately and honestly to the great work of renewing your society and helping to build a better world.

Today's world demands that you be a
protagonist of history because life is always
beautiful when we choose to live it fully, when
we choose to leave a mark. History today
calls us to defend our dignity and not to let
others decide our future.

SOLIDARITY

We Christians were not chosen
by the Lord for little things; push
onwards toward the highest
principles. Stake your lives on
noble ideals.

Change

CHANGE

I wanted to tell you this and say to you, have courage, go forward and make noise. Where there are young people so should there be noise. Then things settle down but the dream of a young person is to make noise forever. Go ahead! In life there will always be people who suggest that you slow down, blocking your path. Please go against the current. Be courageous.

Always being free to choose goodness is demanding but it will make you into people with a backbone who can face life, people with courage and patience.

It is the young who want to be the protagonists of change. Please, don't leave it to others to be the protagonists of change. You are the ones who hold the future!

Try to be *free with regard to material things*. The Lord calls us to a Gospel lifestyle marked by sobriety, by a refusal to yield to the culture of consumerism. This means being concerned with the essentials and learning to do without all those unneeded extras which hem us in. Let us learn to be detached from possessiveness and from the idolatry of money and lavish spending. Let us put Jesus first.

We must protect creation for it is a gift which the Lord has given us, it is God's present to us; we are the guardians of creation. When we exploit creation, we destroy that sign of God's love. To destroy creation is to say to God: "I don't care." And this is not good: this is sin.

I ask you to be builders of the world, to work for a better world. Dear young people, please, don't be observers of life, but get involved. Jesus did not remain an observer, but he immersed himself. Don't be observers, but immerse yourself in the reality of life, as Jesus did.

CHANGE

Situations can change, people can change. Be the first to seek to bring good, do not grow accustomed to evil, but defeat it with good.

Mercy has an ever-youthful face, and
constantly invites us to be part of his
Kingdom, it is a Kingdom of joy, a Kingdom
always joyful, always driving us forward, a
Kingdom able to give us the strength to
change things.

C
H
A
N
G
E

Your young hearts want to build a
better world. I have been closely
following the news reports of
the many young people who
throughout the world have taken to
the streets in order to express their
desire for a more just and fraternal
society. Young people in the streets.

Do not allow yourselves to be robbed of the will to build great and lasting things in your life! This is what leads you forward. Do not content yourselves with little goals. Aspire to happiness, have courage, the courage to go outside of yourselves and bet on the fullness of your future together with Jesus.

PART 2

Faith and
Community

God

Opening ourselves to God is opening ourselves to others. Take a few steps outside ourselves, little steps, but take them. Little steps, going out of yourselves toward God and toward others, opening your heart to brotherhood, to friendship and to solidarity.

Do we feel the restlessness of love? Do we believe in love for God and for others? Not in an abstract manner, not only in words, but as a real brother to those we come across, the brother who is beside us! Are we moved by their needs or do we remain closed in on ourselves?

God created that person in his image, and he or she reflects something of God's glory. Every human being is the object of God's infinite tenderness, and he himself is present in their lives.

On our way of faith it is also important to know and to feel that God loves us and not to be afraid to love him. Faith is professed with the lips and with the heart, with words and with love.

There are no difficulties, trials or misunderstandings to fear, provided we remain united to God as branches to the vine, provided we do not lose our friendship with him, provided we make ever more room for him in our lives. This is especially so whenever we feel poor, weak and sinful, because God grants strength to our weakness, riches to our poverty, conversion and forgiveness to our sinfulness. The Lord is so rich in mercy: every time, if we go to him, he forgives us.

God counts on you for what you are, not for what you possess. In his eyes the clothes you wear or the kind of cell phone you use are of absolutely no concern. He doesn't care whether you are stylish or not; he cares about you, just as you are! In his eyes, you are precious, and your value is inestimable.

Dear brothers and sisters, let us be
enveloped by the mercy of God;
let us trust in his patience, which
always gives us more time. Let us
find the courage to return to his
house, to dwell in his loving wounds,
allowing ourselves be loved by him
and to encounter his mercy in the
sacraments.

Dear friends, let us open wide the door of our lives to the new things of God which the Holy Spirit gives us. May he transform us, confirm us in our trials, strengthen our union with the Lord, our steadfastness in him: this is a true joy!

In my own life, I have so often seen
God's merciful countenance, his
patience; I have also seen so many
people find the courage to enter
the wounds of Jesus by saying to
him: Lord, I am here, accept my
poverty, hide my sin in your wounds,
wash it away with your blood. And
I have always seen that God did just
this—he accepted them, consoled
them, cleansed them, loved them.

If we are to share our lives with others and generously give of ourselves, we also have to realize that every person is worthy of our giving. Not for their physical appearance, their abilities, their language, their way of thinking, or for any satisfaction that we might receive, but rather because they are God's handiwork, his creation.

No single act of love for God will be lost, no generous effort is meaningless, no painful endurance is wasted. All of these encircle our world like a vital force.

Jesus

JESUS

When Jesus touches a young person's heart, he or she becomes capable of truly great things.

Jesus wants to be your friend, your brother,
a teacher of truth and life who reveals to
you the route to follow in order to reach
happiness, the fulfilment of yourselves in
accordance with God's plan for each
one of you.

J
E
S
U
S

Dear young people, love Jesus Christ more and more! Our life is a response to his call and you will be happy and will build your life well if you can answer this call. May you feel the Lord's presence in your life. He is close to each one of you as a companion, as a friend who knows how to help and understand you, who encourages you in difficult times and never abandons you.

Jesus can give you true passion for life. Jesus can inspire us not to settle for less, but to give the very best of ourselves. Jesus challenges us, spurs us on and helps us keep trying whenever we are tempted to give up. Jesus pushes us to keep our sights high and to dream of great things.

JESUS

As far as Jesus is concerned—as the Gospel shows—no one is unworthy of, or far from, his thoughts. No one is insignificant. He loves all of us with a special love; for him all of us are important: *you* are important!

There is a Person who can keep you going, trust in him! It is Jesus! Trust in Jesus! And Jesus is not an illusion! Trust in Jesus. The Lord is always with us. He comes to the shores of the sea of our life, he makes himself close to our failures, our frailty, and our sins in order to transform them. Never stop staking yourselves on him, over and over again.

Jesus' friendship, which brings us the mercy and love of God, is "free," a pure gift. He asks nothing of you in exchange, he only asks you to welcome him. Jesus wants to love you for what you are, even in your frailty and weakness, so that moved by his love, you may be renewed.

Ours is not a joy born of having many possessions, but from having encountered a Person: Jesus, in our midst; it is born from knowing that with him we are never alone, even at difficult moments, even when our life's journey comes up against problems and obstacles that seem insurmountable, and there are so many of them!

JESUS

We accompany, we follow Jesus, but above all we know that he accompanies us and carries us on his shoulders. This is our joy, this is the hope that we must bring to this world.

Jesus loves each one of you, each one of us, with an infinite love! By his death on the cross and his resurrection, he proved his boundless mercy, gave us salvation and opened the way for us to a new life.

Every day we must let Christ transform us and conform us to him; it means striving to live as Christians, endeavouring to follow him in spite of seeing our limitations and weaknesses. The temptation to set God aside in order to put ourselves at the centre is always at the door.

We dilute fruit drinks—orange, apple, or banana juice, but please do not drink a diluted form of faith. Faith is whole and entire, not something that you water down. It is faith in Jesus. It is faith in the Son of God made man, who loved me and who died for me.

The Cross of Christ contains all the love of God; there we find his immeasurable mercy. This is a love in which we can place all our trust, in which we can believe. Dear young people, let us entrust ourselves to Jesus, let us give ourselves over to him, because he never disappoints anyone!

If something should rightly disturb us and trouble our consciences, it is the fact that so many of our brothers and sisters are living without the strength, light and consolation born of friendship with Jesus Christ, without a community of faith to support them, without meaning and a goal in life.

I invite all Christians, everywhere, at this very moment, to a renewed personal encounter with Jesus Christ, or at least an openness to letting him encounter them; I ask all of you to do this unfailingly each day.

We face so many challenges in life: poverty, distress, humiliation, the struggle for justice, persecutions, the difficulty of daily conversion, the effort to remain faithful to our call to holiness, and many others. But if we open the door to Jesus and allow him to be part of our lives, if we share our joys and sorrows with him, then we will experience the peace and joy that only God, who is infinite love, can give.

Following Jesus

FOLLOWING

Dear young people, Jesus is waiting for us. Jesus is counting on us.

To receive Jesus is to have everything;
to give him is to give the greatest
gift of all.

FOLLOWING

Jesus does not want to act alone, he came to bring the love of God into the world and he wants to spread it in the style of communion, in the style of brotherhood. That is why he immediately forms a community of disciples, which is a missionary community. He trains them straight away for the mission, to go forth.

Following Jesus entails giving up evil
and selfishness and choosing good,
truth and justice, even when this
demands sacrifice and the renunciation
of our own interests.

To say that Jesus is alive means to rekindle our enthusiasm in following him, to renew our passionate desire to be his disciples. What better opportunity to renew our friendship with Jesus than by building friendships among yourselves!

We are called to serve the crucified Jesus in
all those who are marginalized, to touch his
sacred flesh in those who are disadvantaged,
in those who hunger and thirst, in the naked
and imprisoned, the sick and unemployed,
in those who are persecuted, refugees and
migrants. There we find our God; there we
touch the Lord.

Jesus is looking at you now and is
asking you: Do you want to help me
carry the Cross? Brothers and sisters,
with all the strength of your youth,
how will you respond to him?

The Cross of Christ invites us also to allow
ourselves to be smitten by his love, teaching
us always to look upon others with mercy
and tenderness, especially those who suffer,
who are in need of help, who need a word or
a concrete action; the Cross invites us to step
outside ourselves to meet them and to extend
a hand to them.

FOLLOWING

Dear brothers and sisters, no one can approach and touch the Cross of Jesus without leaving something of himself or herself there, and without bringing something of the Cross of Jesus into his or her own life.

Let us always remember: young people do not follow the Pope, they follow Jesus Christ, bearing his Cross. And the Pope guides them and accompanies them on this journey of faith and hope.

FOLLOWING

Jesus is not the Lord of comfort, security and ease. Following Jesus demands a good dose of courage, a readiness to trade in the sofa for a pair of walking shoes and to set out on new and uncharted paths.

Let us multiply the works of the culture of acceptance, works inspired by Christian love, love for Jesus crucified, for the flesh of Christ. To serve with love and tenderness persons who need our help makes all of us grow in humanity. It opens before us the way to eternal life. Those who engage in works of mercy have no fear of death.

Jesus wants us to touch human misery, to touch the suffering flesh of others. He hopes that we will stop looking for those personal or communal niches which shelter us from the maelstrom of human misfortune and instead enter into the reality of other people's lives and know the power of tenderness.

Now each one of you could ask: How am I experiencing "being" with Jesus? This is a question I leave you: "How do I experience this remaining with Jesus, abiding in Jesus? Do I find time to remain in his presence, in silence, to be looked upon by him? Do I let his fire warm my heart? If the warmth of God, of his love, of his tenderness is not in our own hearts, then how can we, who are poor sinners, warm the heart of others?"

FOLLOWING

As disciples of Christ, we have
a further reason to join with all
men and women of good will to
protect and defend nature and the
environment.

Prayer

PRAYER

Speak continually with Jesus, in the good times and in the bad, when you do right, and when you do wrong. Do not fear him!
This is prayer.

In order to speak to others about Jesus it is necessary to know and love him, to experience him in prayer, in listening to his word.

PRAYER

In prayer, in conversation with him
and in reading the Bible you will
discover that he is truly close. You
will also learn to read God's signs
in your life. He always speaks to us,
also through the events of our time
and our daily life; it is up to us to
listen to him.

Among the many things to do in our daily *routine*, one of the priorities, should be reminding ourselves of our Creator who allows us to live, who loves us, who accompanies us on our journey.

PRAYER

Dear friends, let us bring to Christ's
Cross our joys, our sufferings and
our failures. There we will find
a Heart that is open to us and
understands us, forgives us, loves us
and calls us to bear this love in
our lives, to love each person,
each brother and sister, with the
same love.

It will do us good to pray every morning:
"Lord, I thank you for loving me; I am sure
that you love me; help me to be in love
with my own life!" Not with my faults, that
need to be corrected, but with life itself,
which is a great gift, for it is a time
to love and to be loved.

PRAYER

It is the Word of God that continually renews our hearts and our communities. Therefore, let us not forget to read it and meditate upon it every day, so that it may become for each like a flame that we bear inside us to illuminate our steps, as well as those of others who journey beside us, who are perhaps struggling to find the path to Christ.

Another good way to grow in friendship with Christ is by listening to his word. The Lord speaks to us in the depths of our conscience, he speaks to us through Sacred Scripture, he speaks to us in prayer. Learn to stay before him in silence, to read and meditate on the Bible, especially the Gospels, to converse with him every day in order to feel his presence of friendship and love.

In Holy Mass we celebrate the memorial of the Lord's sacrifice, his total gift of himself for our salvation: still today he really gives his Body for us and pours out his Blood to redeem humanity's sins and to bring us into communion with him.

Dear young friends, don't be ashamed to bring everything to the Lord in confession, especially your weaknesses, your struggles and your sins. He will surprise you with his forgiveness and his peace.

PRAYER

In Penance, Jesus accepts us with all our limitations, he brings us the mercy of the Father who forgives us and transforms our heart, making it a new heart that can love as he does, as he who loved his own to the end (cf. John 13:1). Moreover this love is expressed in his mercy. Jesus always pardons us.

Believing Together

BELIEVING

To those who feel far from God and the Church, to all those who are fearful or indifferent, I would like to say this: the Lord, with great respect and love, is also calling you to be a part of his people!

The Lord needs you, young people, for his Church. My friends, the Lord needs you! Today too, he is calling each of you to follow him in his Church and to be missionaries. The Lord is calling you today! Not the masses, but you, and you, and you, each one of you. Listen to what he is saying to you in your heart.

BELIEVING

We are not isolated and we are not Christians on an individual basis, each one on his or her own, no, *our Christian identity is to belong!* We are Christians because we belong to the Church.

Today Christ is knocking at the door of your heart, of my heart. He calls you and me to rise, to be wide awake and alert, and to see the things in life that really matter. What is more, he is asking you and me to go out on the highways and byways of this world, knocking on the doors of other people's hearts, inviting them to welcome him into their lives.

BELIEVING

What is the mission of the Church? To spread throughout the world the flame of faith which Jesus kindled in the world: faith in God who is Father, Love, Mercy.

The mission also helps us to look at each other, in the eyes, and to recognize that *we are brothers*, there is not a city or even a Church of the good and a city or a Church of the bad.

BELIEVING

As young Christians, whether you are workers or students, whether you have already begun a career or have answered the call to marriage, religious life or the priesthood, you are not only a part of the *future* of the Church; you are also a necessary and beloved part of the Church's *present*!

I want a Church which is poor and for the poor. They have much to teach us.

BELIEVING

Jesus is asking us to build up his Church; each one of us is a living stone, a small part of the edifice; when the rain comes, if this piece is missing, there are leaks and water comes in. Don't build a little chapel which holds only a small group of persons. Jesus asks us to make his living Church so large that it can hold all of humanity, that it can be a home for everyone!

Indeed, I hoped that increasing space may be offered to women for a more widespread and incisive presence in the Church.

BELIEVING

The Church is meant to be a seed
of unity for the whole human family.
In Christ, all nations and peoples
are called to a unity which does not
destroy diversity but acknowledges,
reconciles and enriches it.

We are all children of God. All sinners and all with the Holy Spirit within, that has the capacity to make us saints.

BELIEVING

Let us encourage the generosity
which is typical of the young
and help them to work actively
in building a better world. Young
people are a powerful engine for the
Church and for society.

Keeping the doors of our churches open also means keeping them open in the digital environment so that people, whatever their situation in life, can enter, and so that the Gospel can go out to reach everyone. We are called to show that the Church is the home of all.

BELIEVING

To be Church is to feel oneself in the hands of God, who is father and loves us, caresses us, waits for us and makes us feel His tenderness. And this is very beautiful!

We are the community of believers, we are the People of God and in this community we share the beauty of the experience of a love that precedes us all, but that at the same time calls us to be "channels" of grace for one another, despite our limitations and our sins.

B
E
L
I
E
V
I
N
G

In the Church, there are a variety of vocations and a variety of spiritualties. What is important is to find the way best suited for you to be with the Lord, and this everyone can do; it is possible for every state of life.

Living Faith

The method of Christian mission is not proselytism but rather that of sharing the flame that warms the soul.

Teenagers and young people play a special
role: you are called to speak about Jesus
to your peers, not only within the parish
community or your association, but most of
all beyond it. This is a commitment especially
reserved to you, because with your courage,
your enthusiasm, spontaneity and ease of
getting together, you are more easily able to
reach the mind and heart of those who have
distanced themselves from the Lord.

L
I
V
I
N
G

Together with young people everywhere, you want to help build a world where we all live together in peace and friendship, overcoming barriers, healing divisions, rejecting violence and prejudice. And this is exactly what God wants for us.

So many teenagers and young people your age have an immense need of someone who through their own life tells them that Jesus knows us, that Jesus loves us, that Jesus forgives us, shares our difficulties with us and supports us with his grace.

We cannot keep ourselves shut up in parishes, in our communities, in our parish or diocesan institutions, when so many people are waiting for the Gospel! To go out as ones sent. It is not enough simply to open the door in welcome because they come, but we must go out through that door to seek and meet the people!

Let us respond, not like those who push away people who make demands on us, as if serving the needy gets in the way of our being close to the Lord. No! We are to be like Christ, who responds to every plea for his help with love, mercy and compassion.

L
I
V
I
N
G

A merciful heart is able to be a
place of refuge for those who are
without a home or have lost their
home; it is able to build a home and
a family for those forced to emigrate;
it knows the meaning of tenderness
and compassion.

A merciful heart can share its bread with the hungry and welcome refugees and migrants. To say the word "mercy" along with you is to speak of opportunity, future, commitment, trust, openness, hospitality, compassion and dreams.

I recalled the indispensable contribution which women make to society, particularly through the sensitivity and intuition they show to others, the weak and the vulnerable.

Each individual Christian and every community is called to be an instrument of God for the liberation and promotion of the poor, and for enabling them to be fully a part of society.

L
I
V
I
N
G

Today more than ever we feel the need to take the way of ecumenism by inviting others to a true dialogue that looks for elements of truth and goodness and that offers answers inspired by the Gospel. The Holy Spirit urges us to come out of ourselves to meet others!

Let us boldly become citizens of the digital world. The Church needs to be concerned for, and present in, the world of communication, in order to dialogue with people today and to help them encounter Christ. She needs to be a Church at the side of others, capable of accompanying everyone along the way.

L
I
V
I
N
G

Christians have the duty to proclaim the Gospel without excluding anyone. Instead of seeming to impose new obligations, they should appear as people who wish to share their joy, who point to a horizon of beauty and who invite others to a delicious banquet.

We are all called to offer ourselves to the Father with Jesus and like Jesus, making a generous gift of our life, in the family, at work, in service to the Church, in works of mercy.

I want you to make yourselves heard
in your dioceses, I want the noise to
go out, I want the Church to go out
onto the streets, I want us to resist
everything worldly, everything static,
everything comfortable, everything
to do with clericalism, everything
that might make us closed in on
ourselves. The parishes, the schools,
the institutions are made for going
out…if they don't, they become an
NGO, and the Church cannot be an
NGO. May the bishops and priests
forgive me if some of you create a
bit of confusion afterwards. That's
my advice. Thanks for whatever
you can do.

PART 3

Vocation

Learn to Live

LIVE

Going to school means opening
one's mind and heart to reality,
in the wealth of its aspects, of its
dimensions.

School is one of the educational environments in which we develop through learning how to live, how to become grown-up, mature men and women who can travel, who can follow the road of life. How does school help you to grow? It helps you not only by developing your intelligence, but also by an integral formation of all the aspects of your personality.

In your schools you take part in
various activities that accustom you
to not retreating into yourselves
or into your own small world, but
rather to being open to others,
especially the poorest and neediest.
They accustom you to working hard
to improve the world in which we
live. Be men and women with others
and for others: true champions at
the service of others.

The essential of university life lies in studying, in the effort and patience of thinking which reveals man's tension toward truth, good, beauty. Be aware that by studying you receive a fertile opportunity to recognize and give voice to the loftiest aspirations harboured in your heart, the opportunity to develop them.

To study serves to support a specific vocation. For this reason, university life is dynamism directed and characterized by research and by fraternal sharing. Make the most of this opportune time and study hard and consistently, always open to others.

Do not be content with partial truths or reassuring illusions, but through study embrace an ever fuller understanding of reality. In order to do this it is necessary to listen with humility and to gaze with foresight.

LIVE

Studying is not taking possession of reality in order to manipulate it, but allowing it to speak to us and to reveal something to us, very often even about ourselves; and reality does not allow itself to be understood without the willingness to refine one's perspective, to look at it with new eyes. Thus, study with courage and with hope.

Being Human

HUMAN

The Lord has a vocation for each of us, that place where He wants us to live our life. But we must search for it, find it, and then continue forward.

In calling you God says to you: "You are important to me, I love you, I am counting on you." Jesus says this to each one of us! Joy is born from that! The joy of the moment in which Jesus looked at me. Understanding and hearing this is the secret of our joy. Feeling loved by God, feeling that for him we are not numbers but people; and we know that it is he who is calling us.

HUMAN

We are all called to be saints!

God calls you to make definitive choices, and he has a plan for each of you: to discover that plan and to respond to your vocation is to move toward personal fulfilment. God calls each of us to be holy, to live his life, but he has a particular path for each one of us.

Dear young people, some of you may not yet know what you will do with your lives. Ask the Lord, and he will show you the way. The young Samuel kept hearing the voice of the Lord who was calling him, but he did not understand or know what to say, yet with the help of the priest Eli, in the end he answered: Speak, Lord, for I am listening (cf. 1 Sam 3:1–10). You too can ask the Lord: What do you want me to do? What path am I to follow?

It is important not to turn in on ourselves, burying our own talent, our spiritual, intellectual, and material riches, everything that the Lord has given us, but, rather to open ourselves, to be supportive, to be attentive to others.

God expects something from you,
God wants something from you. God
hopes in you.

God comes to break down all our fences. He comes to open the doors of our lives, our dreams, our ways of seeing things. God comes to break open everything that keeps you closed in. He is encouraging you to dream. He wants to make you see that, with you, the world can be different.

HUMAN

Life is not given to us to be jealously guarded for ourselves, but is given to us so that we may give it in turn. Dear young people, have a deep spirit! Do not be afraid to dream of great things!

Today Jesus, who is the way, the truth and the life, is calling you, you, and you to leave your mark on history. He, who is life, is asking each of you to leave a mark that brings life to your own history and that of many others. He, who is truth, is asking you to abandon the paths of rejection, division and emptiness.

Do not live for yourselves, do not live for yourselves, but live to go forth and do good! There are many young people today in the Square: think of this, ask yourselves this: Is Jesus calling me to go forth, to come out of myself to do good? To you, young people, to you boys and girls I ask: You, are you brave enough for this, do you have the courage to hear the voice of Jesus?

Listen carefully to this: learn to look. *Learn to look with new eyes*, because with the mission, our eyes are renewed. Learn to look at the city, our life, our family, all that there is around us. The missionary experience opens our eyes and our heart: learn to look also with the heart. And in this way, we stop being, permit me the word, *tourists in life*, so as to become men and women, young people who love with commitment in life.

Where does Jesus send us? There are no borders, no limits: he sends us to everyone. The Gospel is for everyone, not just for some. It is not only for those who seem closer to us, more receptive, more welcoming. It is for everyone.

The fact is, unless you offer the best of yourselves, the world will never be different. This is the challenge.

The Lord wants to work one of
the greatest miracles we can
experience; he wants to turn
your hands, my hands, our hands,
into signs of reconciliation, of
communion, of creation. He wants
your hands to continue building
the world of today. And he wants to
build that world with you.

To love one's work, to be present in
difficulties, to feel involved and to respond
responsibly and to arouse that love that each
one of us has in our heart, because the Spirit
has given it to us. Taking the initiative is the
reaction to this summons which is typical
of love.

HUMAN

In the heart of every man and woman is the desire for a full life, including that irrepressible longing for fraternity which draws us to fellowship with others and enables us to see them not as enemies or rivals, but as brothers and sisters to be accepted and embraced.

Your vocation makes you *interested* in every
man and in his deeper issues which are often
left unexpressed or masked. By the strength of
the love of God which you have encountered
and come to know, you are capable of
sympathy and tenderness. Thus, you can be
close enough to *touch* the other, his wounds
and his expectations, his questions and
his needs, with the tenderness that is an
expression of care that erases all distances.

There are many young people today….I would like to ask you: Have you sometimes heard the Lord's voice, in a desire, in a worry, did he invite you to follow him more closely? Have you heard him?… Have you wanted to be apostles of Jesus? We must bet on youth for the great ideals.…Ask Jesus what he wants of you and be brave! Be brave! Ask him this!

Let us also recognize our truest destiny,
our deepest vocation: to be loved, to be
transformed by love, to be transformed by the
beauty of God.

Jesus told us: where your treasure is, there will be your heart—and I ask you: Where is your treasure? What is the most important reality for you, the most precious reality, the one that attracts your heart like a magnet? What attracts your heart? May I say that it is God's love? Do you wish to do good to others, to live for the Lord and for your brothers and sisters?

It is precisely in living with love and offering one's own Christian witness in everyday affairs that we are called to become saints. And each in the conditions and the state of life in which he or she finds him- or herself.

HUMAN

Holiness is a vocation for everyone. Thus we are all called to walk on the path of holiness, and this path has a name and a face: the face of Jesus Christ. He teaches us to become saints.

The Gospel intends to tell us that the
Christian is someone who has a great desire,
a deep desire within him: to meet his Lord
with his brothers and sisters, his travelling
companions.

Charisms—that word is a little difficult—are gifts that the Holy Spirit gives us, talents, possibilities….Gifts given not to be hidden but to be shared with others. They are not given for the benefit of the one who receives them, but for the use of the People of God.

I am a mission on this earth; that is the reason why I am here in this world. We have to regard ourselves as sealed, even branded, by this mission of bringing light, blessing, enlivening, raising up, healing and freeing.

HUMAN

This doctrine of our faith is an even stronger stimulus for us to have a responsible and respectful relationship with Creation: in inanimate nature, in plants and in animals, we recognize the imprint of the Creator, and in our fellow kind, His very image.

All Christians, insofar as they have been baptized, are equal in dignity before the Lord and share in the same vocation, that is, to sainthood.

God Is Calling

CALLING

Therefore every vocation, even within the variety of paths, always requires an exodus from oneself in order to center one's life on Christ and on his Gospel. Both in married life and in the forms of religious consecration, as well as in priestly life, we must surmount the ways of thinking and acting that do not conform to the will of God. It is an "exodus that leads us on a journey of adoration of the Lord and of service to him in our brothers and sisters."

Becoming a priest or a man or woman
religious is not primarily our own decision.
I do not trust that seminarian or that woman
novice who says: "I have chosen this path."
I do not like this! It won't do! Rather it is the
response to a call and to a call of love. I hear
something within me which moves me
and I answer "yes."

CALLING

Prayer is needed so that many young people may answer "yes" to the Lord who is calling them to consecrate themselves totally to him for selfless service to their brothers and sisters; to consecrate one's life in order to serve God and the brethren.

Vocations are born in prayer and from prayer;
and only through prayer can they persevere
and bear fruit.

CALLING

It is God who calls; however, it is important to have a daily relationship with him, to listen to him in silence before the Tabernacle and deep within ourselves, to speak with him, to draw near to the sacraments. Having this familiar relationship with the Lord is like keeping the window of our lives open so that he can make us hear his voice and hear what he wants us to do.

Behind and before every vocation to the priesthood or to the consecrated life there is always the strong and intense prayer of someone: a grandmother, a grandfather, a mother, a father, a community.

CALLING

This journey means meditating
on the Gospel every day, in order
to transmit it by your life and
preaching; it means experiencing
the mercy of God in the Sacrament
of Reconciliation. Never omit this!
Always go to confession! And thus
shall you become generous and
merciful ministers because you will
feel God's mercy upon you. It means
nourishing yourselves with faith
and love for the Eucharist, in order
to nourish the Christian people;
it means being men of prayer so
as to become the voice of Christ
praising the Father and interceding
continually for the brethren.

It is not enough just to read the Sacred
Scriptures, we need to listen to Jesus who
speaks in them: it is Jesus himself who speaks
in the Scriptures, it is Jesus who speaks in
them. We need to be receiving antennas that
are tuned into the Word of God, in order to
become broadcasting antennas!

CALLING

Jesus directs us to a one-way street: that of going forth from ourselves. It is a one-way trip, with no return ticket. It involves making an exodus from ourselves, losing our lives for his sake and setting out on the path of self-gift.

What does Jesus ask of us? He desires hearts that are truly consecrated, hearts that draw life from His forgiveness in order to pour it out with compassion on our brothers and sisters. Jesus wants hearts that are open and tender towards the weak, never hearts that are hardened.

To go forth, go forth! For me this is the kernel of evangelization. And going forth means going somewhere, i.e., closeness. If you don't go out of yourself you will never reach closeness! Closeness. To be close to people, to be close to everyone, to all those to whom we should be close. All people. Go forth. Closeness. One cannot evangelize without closeness! Closeness with kindness; the closeness of love, also physical closeness; to be close to another.

A vocation is a fruit that ripens in a well cultivated field of mutual love that becomes mutual service, in the context of an authentic ecclesial life. No vocation is born of itself or lives for itself. A vocation flows from the heart of God and blossoms in the good soil of faithful people, in the experience of fraternal love.

CALLING

Dear brothers and sisters, each of us holds in his or her heart a very personal page of the book of God's mercy. It is the story of our own calling, the voice of the love that attracted us and transformed our life, leading us to leave everything at His word and to follow Him. Today let us gratefully rekindle the memory of His call, which is stronger than any resistance and weariness on our part.

I like comparing the vocation to the ordained ministry to the "treasure hidden in a field." It is truly a treasure that God places from the beginning in the hearts of some men; those whom He has chosen and called to follow him in this special state of life. This treasure, which needs to be discovered and brought to light, is not meant to "enrich" just someone. The one called to the ministry is not the "master" of his vocation, but the administrator of a gift that God has entrusted to him for the good of all people, rather, of all men and women, including those who have distanced themselves from religious practice or do not profess faith in Christ.

CALLING

The Church and the world need this testimony of the love and mercy of God. The consecrated, men and women religious, are the testimony that God is good and merciful.

Let us give thanks to the Lord that our Church has so many missionaries, she has had so many missionaries, yet she needs even more! Let us thank the Lord for this. Perhaps among so many young people, teenagers who are here, someone has the will to become a missionary: go ahead! This is beautiful, to spread the Gospel of Jesus. Be brave young people!

A priest or a man or woman
religious can never be an island,
but must be a person who is always
ready to meet others.

Love One Another

ANOTHER

Be a saint by carrying out your work with honesty and competence and by offering time in the service of your brothers and sisters.

I like to think that a synonym, another name
that we Christians could be called is this: we
are men and women, we are a people who
bless. The Christian by his life must bless
always, bless God and bless all people. We
Christians are a people who bless, who know
how to bless. This is a beautiful vocation!

ANOTHER

The Christian cannot keep his faith
hidden, because it shines through in
every word, in every deed, even the
most simple and mundane: the love
that God has given through Jesus
shines through.

Do not bury your talents! Set your stakes on great ideals, the ideals that enlarge the heart, the ideals of service that make your talents fruitful.

ANOTHER

Humanity today needs men and
women, and especially young
people like yourselves, who do
not wish to live their lives "halfway,"
young people ready to spend their
lives freely in service to those of
their brothers and sisters who are
poorest and most vulnerable, in
imitation of Christ who gave himself
completely for our salvation.

In the face of evil, suffering and sin, the only response possible for a disciple of Jesus is the gift of self, even of one's own life, in imitation of Christ; it is the attitude of service.

ANOTHER

Do not be afraid to go and to bring Christ into every area of life, to the fringes of society, even to those who seem farthest away, most indifferent. The Lord seeks all, he wants everyone to feel the warmth of his mercy and his love.

Dear friends, the Lord once more asks you to be in the forefront of serving others. He wants to make of you *a concrete response* to the needs and sufferings of humanity. He wants you to be signs of his merciful love for our time! To enable you to carry out this mission, he shows you the way of personal commitment and self-sacrifice. It is the Way of the Cross.

ANOTHER

Let us think where I can go to bring a little relief, a little peace, to those who suffer.

Our smallest gesture of love benefits everyone!

ANOTHER

As the Samaritan who *passes by*, *sees* and *takes compassion*. This is the action to which you are committed by your vocation: pass by every man and make yourself a neighbour to every person you meet. Because your permanence in the world is not simply sociological, it is a theological reality that calls you *to be* aware, attentive, that can perceive, see and touch the flesh of his brother.

This is it: every state of life leads to holiness, always! In your home, on the street, at work, at church, in that moment and in your state of life, the path to sainthood has been opened. Don't be discouraged to pursue this path. It is God alone who gives us the grace. The Lord asks only this: that we be in communion with Him and at the service of our brothers and sisters.

This is the vocation of Christ and the vocation of Christians as well. To go to others, to those in need, whether their needs be material or spiritual….Many people who suffer anxiety because of family problems….To bring peace there, to bring the unction of Jesus, the oil of Jesus which does so much good and consoles souls.

I encourage all those who have made the Gospel call to "visit the sick" a personal life decision: physicians, nurses, healthcare workers, chaplains and volunteers. May the Lord help you to do your work well, here as in every other hospital in the world. I cannot fail to mention, here, the work of so many sisters who offer their lives in hospitals. May the Lord reward you by giving you inner peace and a heart always capable of tenderness.

A
N
O
T
H
E
R

Your radio and television network can broadcast something of that voice over the air so that it can speak to the men and women who are looking for a word of hope and reassurance for their lives. In this way you become the voice of a Church that is not afraid to enter into man's deserts, to go out to meet him, to go in search of him in his restlessness, in his dismay, dialoguing with everyone, even with those who, for various reasons, have distanced themselves from the Christian community and feel far from God.

A short time ago, a young farmer testified
to his "vocation" by his choice of pursuing
a degree in agriculture and working the
land. The farmer's staying on the land is
not standing still, it is having a dialogue, a
fruitful dialogue, a creative dialogue. It is
man's dialogue with his land which makes it
blossom, makes it fruitful for all of us.

ANOTHER

Business is a vocation, and a noble vocation, provided that those engaged in it see themselves challenged by a greater meaning in life; this will enable them truly to serve the common good by striving to increase the goods of this world and to make them more accessible to all.

In sports competitions you are called to demonstrate that sport which expresses the joy of life, of games, is a celebration, and as such it must be appreciated through the recovery of its gratuitousness, its capacity to foster the bonds of friendship and strengthen openness between people. Also with your daily behavior, full of faith and spirituality, humanity and altruism, you can render testimony to the ideals of peaceful civil and social coexistence, for the edification of a civilization founded on love, on solidarity and on peace....I ask you all to live sport as a gift from God, an opportunity to make good use of your talents.

ANOTHER

The international business community can count on many men and women of great personal honesty and integrity, whose work is inspired and guided by high ideals of fairness, generosity and concern for the authentic development of the human family. I urge you to draw upon these great human and moral resources and to take up this challenge with determination and far-sightedness. Without ignoring, naturally, the specific scientific and professional requirements of every context, I ask you to ensure that humanity is served by wealth and not ruled by it.

Politics, though often denigrated, remains a lofty vocation and one of the highest forms of charity, inasmuch as it seeks the common good.

Marriage and Family

FAMILY

We are created in order to love, as a reflection of God and his love. And in the marital union man and woman fulfil this vocation through their mutual reciprocity and their full and definitive communion of life.

What is marriage? It is *a true and authentic vocation*, as are the priesthood and the religious life. Two Christians who marry have recognized the call of the Lord in their own love story, the vocation to form one flesh and one life from two, male and female.

F
A
M
I
L
Y

It is as though matrimony were
first a human sacrament, where
the person discovers himself,
understands himself in relation to
others and in a relationship of love
which is capable of receiving
and giving.

True joy comes from a profound harmony between persons, something which we all feel in our hearts and which makes us experience the beauty of togetherness, of mutual support along life's journey.

FAMILY

Spousal and familial love also clearly reveals the vocation of the person to love in a unique way and forever, and that the trials, sacrifices and crises of couples as well as of the family as a whole represent pathways for growth in goodness, truth and beauty.

In marriage we give ourselves completely without calculation or reserve, sharing everything, gifts and hardship, trusting in God's Providence. This is the experience that the young can learn from their parents and grandparents. It is an experience of faith in God and of mutual trust, profound freedom and holiness, because holiness presumes giving oneself with fidelity and sacrifice every day of one's life!

FAMILY

Are you married?—Be a saint by loving and taking care of your husband or your wife, as Christ did for the Church.

When a man and woman celebrate the Sacrament of Matrimony God as it were "is mirrored" in them; he impresses in them his own features and the indelible character of his love.

FAMILY

Each Christian family can first of all—as Mary and Joseph did—welcome Jesus, listen to Him, speak with Him, guard Him, protect Him, grow with Him; and in this way improve the world. Let us make room in our heart and in our day for the Lord.

This is the great mission of the family:
to make room for Jesus who is coming, to
welcome Jesus in the family, in each member:
children, husband, wife, grandparents....
Jesus is there.

F
A
M
I
L
Y

Let us think: How many dads and moms every day put their faith into practice by offering up their own lives in a concrete way for the good of the family?! Think about this!

Be a saint by passionately teaching your children or grandchildren to know and to follow Jesus. And it takes so much patience to do this: to be a good parent, a good grandfather, a good mother, a good grandmother; it takes so much patience and with this patience comes holiness: by exercising patience.

When a young mom or dad comes, I ask: "How many children do you have?" and they tell me. And I ask another question, always: "Tell me: Do you play with your children?" Most of them answer: "What are you asking, Father?"—"Yes, yes: Do you play? Do you spend time with your children?" We are losing this capacity, this wisdom of playing with our children. The economic situation pushes us to this, to lose this. Please, spend time with our children!

The mission of the Christian family, today as yesterday, is that of proclaiming to the world, by the power of the Sacrament of Marriage, the love of God.

FAMILY

When the Lord calls, he always does so for the good of others, whether it is through the religious life, the consecrated life, or as a lay person, as the father or mother of a family. The goal is the same: to worship God and to do good to others.

Christian families are missionary families. Yesterday in this square we heard the testimonies of missionary families. They are missionary also in everyday life, in their doing everyday things, as they bring to everything the salt and the leaven of faith! Keeping the faith in families and bringing to everyday things the salt and the leaven of faith.

Priesthood

PRIESTHOOD

It is so beautiful to find a priest, a
good priest, filled with goodness.

The Lord calls some to be priests, to give
themselves to him more fully, so as to love all
people with the heart of the Good Shepherd.
Some he calls to the service of others in
the religious life: devoting themselves in
monasteries to praying for the good of the
world, and in various areas of the apostolate,
giving of themselves for the sake of all,
especially those most in need.

The Lord calls. He calls each of those whom he wills to become priests. Perhaps there are some young men present here who have heard this call in their hearts, the aspiration to become a priest, the desire to serve others in the things of God, the desire to spend one's entire life in service in order to catechize, baptize, forgive, celebrate the Eucharist, heal the sick…the whole of one's life in this way. If some of you have heard this call in your heart, it is Jesus who has placed it there.

For us priests and consecrated persons, conversion to the newness of the Gospel entails a daily encounter with the Lord in prayer. The saints teach us that this is the source of all apostolic zeal!

P
R
I
E
S
T
H
O
O
D

All who are called should know that genuine and complete joy does exist in this world: it is the joy of being taken from the people we love and then being sent back to them as dispensers of the gifts and counsels of Jesus, the one Good Shepherd who, with deep compassion for all the little ones and the outcasts of this earth, wearied and oppressed like sheep without a shepherd, wants to associate many others to his ministry, so as himself to remain with us and to work, in the person of his priests, for the good of his people.

The life of Jesus' closest disciples, which
is what we are called to be, is shaped by
concrete love, a love, in other words, marked
by service and availability.

PRIESTHOOD

The priest, the bishop, the deacon must shepherd the Lord's flock with love. It is useless if it is not done with love. And in this sense, the ministers who are chosen and consecrated for this service extend Jesus' presence in time, if they do so by the power of the Holy Spirit, in God's name and with love.

Wherever God's people have desires or needs, there is the priest, who knows how to listen… and feels a loving mandate from Christ who sends him to relieve that need with mercy or to encourage those good desires with resourceful charity.

PRIESTHOOD

Through Holy Orders the minister dedicates himself entirely to his community and loves it with all his heart: it is his family. The bishop and the priest love the Church in their own community, they love it greatly. How? As Christ loves the Church. St. Paul will say the same of marriage: the husband is to love his wife as Christ loves the Church. It is a great mystery of love: this of priestly ministry and that of matrimony are two Sacraments, pathways which people normally take to go to the Lord.

Priests must also live in a manner that is consistent with what they preach; the very credibility of the Church's witness is at stake.

PRIESTHOOD

Priests are united in a sacramental
brotherhood, therefore, the first
form of evangelization is the witness
of brotherhood and of communion
among themselves and with their
bishop. From such a communion
can arise a powerful missionary
zeal—which frees ordained
ministers from the comfortable
temptation of being over anxious
about the opinion of others and of
their own well being, than inspired
by pastoral love—in order to
proclaim the Gospel, to the remotest
peripheries.

Disciples do not hesitate to ask questions,
they have the courage to face their misgivings
and bring them to the Lord.

PRIESTHOOD

I repeat it often: walking with
our people, sometimes in front,
sometimes behind and sometimes
in the middle…: in front in order to
guide the community, in the middle
in order to encourage and support;
and at the back in order to keep it
united and so that no one lags too,
too far behind, to keep them united.

We must find the Lord who consoles us and go to console the people of God. This is the mission. People today certainly need words, but most of all they need us to bear witness to the mercy and tenderness of the Lord, which warms the heart, rekindles hope, and attracts people towards the good. What a joy it is to bring God's consolation to others!

PRIESTHOOD

Every vocation is missionary and
the mission of ordained ministers is
evangelization, in all its forms.
It starts in the first place with
"being," in order to then be
translated into "doing."

Be present to those who, living in the midst
of a society burdened by poverty and
corruption, are broken in spirit, tempted
to give up, to leave school and to
live on the streets.

PRIESTHOOD

I would like to say a special word
to the young priests, religious and
seminarians among us. I ask you
to share the joy and enthusiasm of
your love for Christ and the Church
with everyone, but especially with
your peers. Be present to young
people who may be confused and
despondent, yet continue to see
the Church as their friend on the
journey and a source of hope.

Religious Life

Family life is the vocation that God inscribed into the nature of man and woman and there is another vocation which is complementary to marriage: *the call to celibacy and virginity for the sake of the Kingdom of Heaven*. It is the vocation that Jesus himself lived.

The consecrated, men and women religious,
are the testimony that God is good and
merciful. Thus it is necessary to appreciate
with gratitude the experiences of consecrated
life and to deepen our understanding of the
different charisms and spiritualities.

Religious men and women are
prophets. They are those who have
chosen a following of Jesus that
imitates his life in obedience to the
Father, poverty, community life and
chastity.

"Being with" Christ does not mean isolating ourselves from others. Rather, it is a "being with" in order to go forth and encounter others. Here I wish to recall some words of Blessed Mother Teresa of Calcutta. She said: "We must be very proud of our vocation because it gives us the opportunity to serve Christ in the poor. It is in the *favelas*,…in the *villas miseria*, that one must go to seek and to serve Christ.

Women have much to say to us in today's society. Sometimes we are too "machista"; we don't make room for women. Women are able to see things differently than men. Women can ask questions that we men just don't get. Pay attention.

For religious, living the newness of the Gospel also means finding ever anew in community life and community apostolates the incentive for an ever closer union with the Lord in perfect charity.

Thanks be to God, you do not live or work as isolated individuals but as a community: and thank God for this! The community supports the whole of the apostolate. At times religious communities are fraught with *tensions*, and risk becoming individualistic and scattered, whereas what is needed is deep communication and authentic relationships. The humanizing power of the Gospel is witnessed in *fraternity lived* in community and is created through welcome, respect, mutual help, understanding, kindness, forgiveness and joy.

For us who are disciples, it is important to put our humanity in contact with the flesh of the Lord, to bring to him, with complete trust and utter sincerity, our whole being.

Love means having the ability to hold a dirty hand and the ability to look into the eyes of those who are in a situation of degradation and say: "For me, you are Jesus." And this is the beginning of every mission, with this love I must go and speak.

For you, as men and women consecrated to God, this joy is rooted in the mystery of the Father's mercy revealed in Christ's sacrifice on the cross. Whether the charism of your Institute is directed more to contemplation or to the active life, you are challenged to become "experts" in divine mercy precisely through your life in community.

From experience I know that community life is not always easy, but it is a providential training ground for the heart. It is unrealistic not to expect conflicts; misunderstandings will arise and they must be faced. Despite such difficulties, it is in community life that we are called to grow in mercy, forbearance and perfect charity.

Never, never let there be envy, jealousy, among you—do not permit these things! And unity at home. The greatest danger is terrorism in religious life: it has entered, the terrorism of gossip. If you have something against a sister, go and tell her to her face. But never this terrorism, because gossip is a bomb thrown into a community and it destroys it.

Women religious should be ready to tackle the difficult and demanding tasks and missions that fulfil their intellectual capacities, their talents and personal charisms. Let us pray for female vocations and let us accompany and esteem our sisters, who often in silence and unnoticed spend their lives for the Lord and for the Church, in prayer, in pastoral care and in charity.

In the Church, the religious are called to be prophets in particular by demonstrating how Jesus lived on this earth, and to proclaim how the kingdom of God will be in its perfection. A religious must never give up prophecy.

LIFE

The consecrated are a sign of God in the different areas of life, they are leaven for the growth of a more just and fraternal society, they are the prophecy of sharing with the least and the poor. Thus understood and lived, consecrated life appears as what it really is: a gift from God, a gift of God to the Church, a gift of God to his People!

Every consecrated person is a gift for the
People of God on it's [*sic*] journey. There
is a great need for their presence, which
strengthens and renews commitment to:
spreading the Gospel, Christian education,
love for the needy, contemplative prayer;
commitment to human formation, the
spiritual formation of young people,
and families; commitment to justice and
peace in the human family.

L
I
F
E

But let us think a little about what
would happen if there were no
sisters in hospitals, no sisters in
missions, no sisters in schools. Think
about a Church without sisters!
It is unthinkable: they are this gift,
this leaven that carries forward the
People of God. These women who
consecrate their life to God, who
carry forward Jesus' message,
are great.

Appendix

Prayers for Discernment

Breathe into me, Holy Spirit,
that my thoughts may all be holy.

Move in me, Holy Spirit,
that my work too, may be holy.

Attract my heart, Holy Spirit,
that I may love only what is holy.

Strengthen me, Holy Spirit,
that I may defend all that is holy.

Protect me, Holy Spirit,
that I may always be holy.

+ St. Augustine

O Holy Spirit,
Shed your light upon my heart.
Teach me to know and understand your hidden
    ways.
Assist my study by bringing your divine wisdom to
    my aid
So that I may learn to know and love you
Whose glory shines through all your works.
I ask this in the name of Jesus our Lord.

+ Fr. Louis O'Hara, CSP

Take, Lord, and receive all my liberty,
my memory, my understanding,
and my entire will,
All I have and call my own.

You have given all to me.
To you, Lord, I return it.

Everything is yours; do with it what you will.
Give me only your love and your grace,
that is enough for me.

+ St. Ignatius of Loyola

My Lord God, I have no idea where I am going.
I do not see the road ahead of me.
I cannot know for certain where it will end.
Nor do I really know myself,
and the fact that I think that I am following your will
does not mean that I am actually doing so.
But I believe that the desire to please you does in
fact please you.
And I hope I have that desire in all that I am doing.
I hope that I will never do anything apart from that
desire.
And I know that if I do this you will lead me by the
right road,
though I may know nothing about it.
Therefore, will I trust you always,
though I may seem to be lost and in the shadow of
death.
I will not fear, for you are ever with me,
and you will never leave me to face my perils alone.

+ Thomas Merton, OCSO

Father, I abandon myself into your hands; do with
    me what you will.
Whatever you may do, I thank you:
I am ready for all, I accept all.
Let only your will be done in me, and in all your
    creatures.
I wish no more than this, O Lord.
Into your hands I commend my soul;
I offer it to you
with all the love of my heart,
for I love you, Lord,
and so need to give myself,
to surrender myself into your hands,
without reserve,
and with boundless confidence,
for you are my Father.

+ Charles de Foucauld

Above all, trust in the slow work of God.
We are quite naturally impatient in everything
to reach the end without delay.
We should like to skip the intermediate stages.
We are impatient of being on the way to
     something
unknown, something new.
And yet it is the law of all progress
that it is made by passing through
some stages of instability—
and that it may take a very long time.

And so I think it is with you;
your ideas mature gradually—let them grow,
let them shape themselves, without undue haste.
Don't try to force them on,
as though you could be today what time
(that is to say, grace and circumstances
acting on your own good will)
will make of you tomorrow.

Only God could say what this new spirit
gradually forming within you will be.
Give Our Lord the benefit of believing
that his hand is leading you,
and accept the anxiety of feeling yourself
in suspense and incomplete.

+ Pierre Teilhard de Chardin

My soul proclaims the greatness of the Lord,
My Spirit rejoices in God my Savior
For He has looked with favor on His lowly servant.

From this day all generations will call me blessed:
The Almighty has done great things for me,
And holy is His Name.

He has mercy on those who fear Him
In every generation.

He has shown the strength of His arm,
He has scattered the proud in their conceit.

He has cast down the mighty from their thrones,
And has lifted up the lowly.

He has filled the hungry with good things,
And the rich He has sent away empty.

He has come to the help of His servant Israel
For He has remembered His promise of mercy,
The promise He made to our fathers,
To Abraham and his children forever.

Canticle of Mary (Luke 1:46–55)

God has created me to do Him some definite
    service;
He has committed some work to me which He has
not committed to another.
I have my mission—I may never know it in this life,
but I shall be told it in the next....
I am a link in a chain,
a bond of connection between persons
He has not created me for naught.
I shall do good, I shall do His work;
I shall be an angel of peace,
a preacher of truth in my own place, while not
intending it, if I do but keep His commandments....
Therefore I will trust Him whatever, wherever I am,
I can never be thrown away.
If I am in sickness, my sickness may serve Him;
In perplexity, my perplexity may serve Him;
If I am in sorrow, my sorrow may serve Him....
He does nothing in vain...
He knows what He is about.
He may take away my friends,

He may throw me among strangers,
He may make me feel desolate,
make my spirits sink, hide the future from me—
still He knows what He is about.

> "Some Definite Purpose" by
> Cardinal John Henry Newman

Helpful Reading from Paulist Press

Becoming Who You Are: Insights on the True Self from Thomas Merton and Other Saints, James Martin, SJ, $11.00

No Journey Will Be Too Long: Friendship in Christian Life, Jose Tolentino Mendonca, $19.95

Pope Francis Talks to Couples: Wisdom on Marriage and Family, Pope Francis, $7.95

Understanding Jesus: 50 Reasons Why Jesus Matters, Andrew Hamilton, SJ, $15.95

What Are We Doing on Earth for Christ's Sake, Richard Leonard, SJ, $14.95

What Does It All Mean: Faith's Big Questions,
Richard Leonard, SJ, $24.95
**Would I Like Jesus: A Casual Walk through the
Life of Jesus**, Peter Fleming, $14.95